Dear Singles
L.I.V.E

A devotional encouraging singles to live intentionally, victoriously, and expectantly

Dr. Ashlei N. Evans

Copyright © 2021 Ashlei N. Evans

To contact the author visit: www.theashexchange.com

All rights reserved. No part of this publication may be reproduced, distributed, or transmitted in any form or by any means, including photocopying, recording, or other electronic or mechanical methods, without the prior written permission of the publisher, except in the case of brief quotations embodied in critical reviews and certain other noncommercial uses permitted by copyright law.

Scripture quotations identified as "AMP" are from the Amplified® Bible, Copyright © 1954, 1958, 1962, 1964, 1965, 1987 by The Lockman Foundation Used by permission." (www.Lockman.org).

Photo by © Andrea Pa Photography

Dedication

Single and never married, single and divorced, single and widowed, single with children, single and not desiring marriage...Whatever stage of singleness you're in, know that there is purpose tied to this season. Don't diminish it, don't despise it, and don't try to rush out of it. Instead, commit to living intentionally, victoriously, and expectant of all that God desires to do in and through you.

TABLE OF CONTENTS

Dedication..Iii
Foreword..Vii
Introduction..Ix
Day 1 - Priorities...1
Day 2 - Identity...7
Day 3 - Purpose...15
Day 4 - Love..23
Day 5 - Sexual Purity..31
Day 6 - Submission..39
Day 7 - Healing..45
Day 8 - Positioning..53
Day 9 - Community (Friendship/Accountability)............61
Day 10 - Purpose Over Preference................................69
Day 11 - Marriage..75
Words to the Wise...83
More from Dr. Ashlei N. Evans..................................101

Foreword

Singleness is a passport, not a prison. That's one thing that we the Flowers' had to learn in our own personal lives prior to marriage. This is one of the reasons why we formed our ministry RedefinedTV. We wanted people to value whatever season God had them in, single or married, and maximize it. Furthermore, we wanted singles to know how necessary and vital it is for an individual to discover their purpose, so that they can live on purpose and be fulfilled completely in purpose. So, if they desire marriage, they can pick on purpose! Dr. Ashlei Evans does a phenomenal job of shedding so much light and insight on this very topic, how to completely enjoy and embrace this time in your life! Because, it is right where God wants you to be! The way she dives into each topic that singles face so efficiently will leave you blessed, encouraged, and with many of your questions answered. We truly believe she articulates God's heart and desires for the unmarried in this devotional. I hope you are ready because your attitude is about to shift for the better!

Pastor Jerry and Tanisha Flowers
Lead Pastors, Time of Celebration Ministries Church
Founders, RedefinedTV

Introduction

Why are you single? This is a common question that can have a variety of responses, but the one I need you to be set free from is that you're single because something is wrong with you or you're doing something wrong. The reality is, there is no secret formula to escape the perceived dreadful season of singleness. I say perceived because singleness is not dreadful but with a skewed perspective, you will treat it like it's the worst thing that has ever happened to you. Singleness is a season that happens for us. It gives us the space to grow in identity, purpose, community, and if it's God's Will for you, it will prepare you to have a healthy perspective when entering a marriage. I'm currently 33 years old and I've been single for years. I've had a few situationships here and there, but those still left me living single. During these years I've gained a great deal of insight as it relates to understanding the significance of singleness and the benefits of singleness when done well.

Ultimately, I desire for you to finish this devotional ready to L.I.V.E., live intentionally, victoriously, and expectantly. Join me on this 11-day journey filled with reflection, rediscovery, redemption, and revelation. Throughout each devotional, I will be sharing God's word along with personal experiences and biblical wisdom. Each devotional will include a Keeping it L.I.V.E. section dedicated to helping you do the hard work that needs to be done to ensure that you start living intentionally, victoriously, and expectantly. You will also receive guidance in prayer, reflection, and journaling. My prayer is that you would begin to see God move in and through you as we complete each day.

Day 1

PRIORITIES

Dear Singles,

Discontentment is often our greatest struggle while in this season. We could be thriving yet not completely satisfied because we feel as if something or, in this case, someone is missing. We fall into our feelings not realizing our feelings are deceptive and will lead us astray. I will not sit here and diminish the joy of marriage, but I will also not allow you to believe that it should be made a priority. God has been put on the back burner far too often simply because we allowed our desires and the beliefs of society to somehow distract us from keeping the main thing the main thing... making God the priority in our life.

Singleness is not an obstacle to overcome nor a race we must win to make it to the altar. It's a season or state of being that allows us to complete certain assignments God has designated for us. When praying about singles, God has always brought me back to Matthew 6:33.

But first and most importantly seek (aim at, strive after) His kingdom and His righteousness [His way of doing and being right—the attitude and character of God], and all these things will be given to you also.

Having read this I must ask, have we been seeking, aiming at, and striving after God, as we seek, aim at, and strive after marriage or other things of this world? I can honestly say there was a season in my life when I wasn't. There did come a time when my efforts toward everything began to fail as a result of me not seeking God first. I was on a mission to fulfill my own desires, and I needed a perspective shift quickly. I had to come to the knowledge of who God is so that I would know that it is not His will to make us feel like He is withholding something from us. He just needs to know that above all things, He becomes our number one priority.

Keeping It L.I.V.E.

My challenge for you is to go into a quiet space and commune with God. Because we can't physically see Him, we often forget that He yearns to spend time with us. Imagine all the times you've wanted someone's attention, and they never gave it to you. That is how God feels when we choose to chase after everything and everyone but His heart. Use the prayer below to get you started. Use the reflection questions to guide your thinking and take time to journal any thoughts that come to your mind. God created you, so don't be afraid of being transparent and honest with Him about your feelings, struggles, and/or fears.

Guiding Prayer:

Heavenly Father,

Thank you for loving me beyond my lack of reciprocation. Lord, I repent for pursuing things of this world more than Your heart and I ask that You would forgive me for not making You a priority in my life. Father, I ask that You reignite my fire for You and remove anything or anyone that may be hindering me from seeking You. I thank You for showing me mercy and for giving me the grace to grow in You. I give You all the honor, power, and glory in Jesus' name, Amen!

Reflection Questions:

1. What does Matthew 6:33 mean to me?
2. What or who have I allowed to distract me from seeking God?
3. What steps do I need to take to ensure I am intentional about seeking God?

Journal

Day 2

IDENTITY

Dear Singles,

Have you ever paused and thought to yourself, "Who am I?" It seems simple, but I've found that many people don't know how to answer this question. As an educator I've seen students of all ages. One thing I've recognized is that the older an individual gets the less they understand their identity. Especially if they grew up being told who they are based upon the opinions of others. You can spend your entire life defining yourself by what people tell you, your cultural values, what you've observed, or your occupation, but our true identity lies in Christ.

When individuals reach a point of having an identity crisis, they begin to say and do things that really seem out of character. What many people fail to realize is that by not understanding your identity in Christ, you are more susceptible to living a life that God never designed for you to live. You are also more at risk of connecting with people who could do more harm than good. The great thing is that it's never too late to gain an understanding or have a refresher on who we are in Christ. Paul spends much of the New Testament reminding people of their identity in Christ. One of the greatest explanations is found in Ephesians 1:3-14. Paul is speaking to the church of Ephesus.

Blessed and worthy of praise be the God and Father of our Lord Jesus Christ, who has blessed us with every spiritual blessing in the heavenly realms in Christ, just as [in His love] He chose us in Christ [actually selected us for Himself as His own] before the foundation of the world, so that we would be holy [that is, consecrated, set apart for Him, purpose-driven] and blameless in His sight. In love He predestined and lovingly planned for us to be adopted to Himself as [His own] children through Jesus Christ, in accordance with the kind intention and good pleasure of His will— to the praise of His glorious grace and favor, which He so freely bestowed on us in the Beloved [His Son, Jesus Christ]. In Him we have redemption [that is, our deliverance and salvation] through His blood, [which paid the penalty for our sin and resulted in] the forgiveness and complete pardon of our sin, in accordance with the riches of His grace which He lavished on us. In all wisdom and understanding [with practical insight] He made known to us the mystery of His will according to His good pleasure, which He purposed in Christ, with regard to the fulfillment of the times [that is, the end of history, the climax of the ages]—to bring all things together in Christ, [both] things in the heavens and things on the earth. In Him also we have received an inheritance [a destiny—we were claimed by God as His own], having been predestined (chosen, appointed beforehand) according to the purpose of Him who works everything in agreement with the counsel and design of His will, so that we who were the first to hope in Christ [who first put our confidence in Him as our Lord and Savior] would exist to the praise of His glory. In Him, you also, when you heard the word of truth, the good news of your salvation, and [as a result] believed in Him, were stamped with the seal of the promised Holy Spirit [the One promised by Christ] as owned and protected [by God]. The Spirit is the guarantee [the first installment, the pledge, a foretaste] of our inheritance until the redemption of God's own [purchased] possession [His believers], to the praise of His glory.

As you can see, God knew exactly what he was doing when he created us. He was intentional and very strategic. I hope that reading this gave you the same sense of liberation that I feel every time I read it. It's a reminder that you are someone significant and in Him you are amazing.

Keeping It L.I.V.E.

Reread Ephesians 1:3-14 and make a list of everything that reveals who you are in Christ. Take some time to thank God for the revelation of your identity in Him. Ask Him to continue to show and remove the things in your life that you have allowed to define you. Next, respond to the reflection questions, reflect on the scriptures listed below, and create affirmations and declarations. Use the journal space to write down any additional prayers, scriptures, and declarations that you need to write so that you can begin speaking life over yourself.

Ephesians 1:3-14 Revelation List

_____
_____
_____
_____
_____
_____
_____
_____
_____
_____

Guiding Prayer

Heavenly Father,
Thank You so much for opening my eyes to who I am in You. Father forgive me for allowing the things of this world to define me. As Paul prayed in Ephesians 1:17-19, I ask that You would give me the Spirit of wisdom and revelation in the knowledge of You. I pray that the eyes of my heart may be enlightened so that I may know what is the hope of Your calling, what is the wealth of Your glorious inheritance in the saints, and what is the immeasurable greatness of Your power toward us who believe, according to the mighty working of His strength. Father, I thank You for giving me clarity and guiding me back into the knowledge of my identity in You. I give You all the honor, power, and glory in Jesus' name, Amen!

Reflection Questions:

Read the Scriptures below and then begin answering the reflection questions below:

1. Prior to reading this devotional, how did I define myself?

2. How has my view of my identity changed?

3. What steps will I take to walk in my identity in Christ?

Genesis 1:27

So God created man in His own image, in the image and likeness of God He created him; male and female He created them.

1 Peter 2:9

But you are a chosen race, a royal priesthood, a consecrated nation, a [special] people for God's own possession, so that you may proclaim the excellencies [the wonderful deeds and virtues and perfections] of Him who called you out of darkness into His marvelous light.

Jeremiah 1:5

Before I formed you in the womb I knew you [and approved of you as My chosen instrument], And before you were born I consecrated you [to Myself as My own]; I have appointed you as a prophet to the nations.

Psalm 139: 13-17

For it was you who created my inward parts; you knit me together in my mother's womb. I will praise you because I have been remarkably and wondrously made. Your works are wondrous, and I know this very well. My bones were not hidden from you when I was made in secret, when I was formed in the depths of the earth. Your eyes saw me when I was formless; all my days were written in your book and planned before a single one of them began. God, how precious your thoughts are to me; how vast their sum is!

Journal

Day 3

PURPOSE

Dear Singles,

I think it's fascinating how God has given us all a purpose, yet some minimize their existence to just becoming a spouse. We sometimes believe that just because we became saved and started going to church that our sole purpose now is to wait for a spouse. Did you know that even in your singleness there is much purpose to be accomplished through you? Did you know that purpose could help you make life changing decisions in life, such as becoming a spouse? Our whole life is a journey of puzzle pieces being gathered together to form the puzzle of life that God has already planned for us and if it's God's Will for your life part of that journey could be marriage. Sadly, there are many individuals who are simply existing in life and doing things just to survive.

As a follower of Christ, we have been commissioned to spread the good news of Christ. We exist for God's glory and not our own, so it's only right that we would be committed to letting people know who He is. After Jesus rose from the dead, he visited the disciples and gave them specific instructions pertaining to what they were to do while on this earth in Matthew 28:18-20:

Jesus came up and said to them, "All authority (all power of absolute rule) in heaven and on earth has been given to Me. Go therefore and make disciples of all the nations [help the people to learn of Me, believe in Me, and obey My words], baptizing them in the name of the Father and of the Son and of the Holy Spirit, teaching them to observe everything that I have commanded you; and lo, I am with you always [remaining with you perpetually—regardless of circumstance, and on every occasion], even to the end of the age."

In 2 Corinthians 5:17-20, we're called Ministers of Reconciliation and Ambassadors for Christ.

Therefore if anyone is in Christ [that is, grafted in, joined to Him by faith in Him as Savior], he is a new creature [reborn and renewed by the Holy Spirit]; the old things [the previous moral and spiritual condition] have passed away. Behold, new things have come [because spiritual awakening brings a new life]. But all these things are from God, who reconciled us to Himself through Christ [making us acceptable to Him] and gave us the ministry of reconciliation [so that by our example we might bring others to Him], that is, that God was in Christ reconciling the world to Himself, not counting people's sins against them [but canceling them]. And He has committed to us the message of reconciliation [that is, restoration to favor with God]. So we are ambassadors for Christ, as though God were making His appeal through us; we [as Christ's representatives] plead with you on behalf of Christ to be reconciled to God.

As you can see, we were created with the purpose of living for Christ and drawing others to Christ. How we live out our purpose will look different. God has given us each a calling that disperses us out to different fields, locations, and people. Whether you are a custodian, parent, social worker, educator, pharmacist, professional dancer, student, musician, pilot, athlete, corporate executive, etc., your purpose will always be rooted in demonstrating the heart of Christ and telling others about Him so that they too can come to the knowledge of Christ.

Many times, people try to leave this role to individuals who operate within the church, but there are numerous areas of influence in this world that need to be covered by the saints: the church, family, education, government, media, arts & entertainment, business, and medical field. Imagine if all the believers in Christ walked in authority in these areas using the gifts, talents, and abilities received to be the light and show the love of Christ. We would be dominating this world!! Nevertheless, you have been called to one or more of these areas, so please do not dim your light and live to only become a spouse because you will find that even your marriage serves a purpose beyond just having someone to say you are married to. There's purpose in that too, but for now, I need you to focus on you first!

Keeping It L.I.V.E.

Understanding our purpose is so important for us to live our lives with intentionality. We won't ever know all the things God desires to accomplish through us, but we can have a sense of how He desires to use us where He has positioned us. Below are questions that will help you unlock your calling so that you have a better understanding of what you're called to do, where you're called to do it, and who you're called to minister to. Use the prayer to help you think through your responses. After praying and answering the questions, journal about what you are hearing from God.

Guiding Prayer:

Heavenly Father,
Thank You for the intentionality You had when creating me. Thank You for loving and trusting me enough to live on this earth to fulfill a purpose far greater than myself. Father forgive me for the many times that I've allowed myself to live

as if there was no significance tied to what I did or said. As I take steps towards becoming more like Christ, Lord I ask that You give me clear insight into what purpose will look like in my life. Remove any false expectations I've created in my mind based on my own fleshly desires. I surrender my life to You, and I ask that You open my mind, heart, eyes, and ears to recognize the different opportunities You present for me to walk in my calling boldly. I give You all the honor, power, and glory in Jesus' name, Amen!

Reflection Questions:

1. What and/or who do I have compassion for?
2. What talents and abilities do I have?
3. What positive characteristics and personality traits do I embody?
4. What are my strengths?
5. What are my weaknesses?
6. What do I dream about doing often?
7. What type of people do I find myself encouraging?
8. What is God saying to me after answering these questions? (Journal Below)

Journal

Day 4

LOVE

Dear Singles,

*L*ove is a phenomenal topic for a song and is often considered to be a feeling, but what if I told you that society has led us all astray when it comes to the real meaning of love? What we call love is normally infatuation, lust, or a strong desire. Please don't be ashamed, because I've made the mistake of thinking I was in love quite a few times. It's nice to hear it, but the reality is love is something that is shown. God was very clear on how we should actually love ALL people. In 1 John 14:7-8, we are reminded of God's greatest commandment which is for us to love one another.

Beloved, let us love one another, for love is from God, and whoever loves has been born of God and knows God. Anyone who does not love does not know God, because God is love.

What I appreciate about these verses is that they point out the reason so many of us are not loving well…we don't know God, who is love. For some this may be a shock, but let's really pause and evaluate whether we know God or know OF God. For years I went to church and fellowshipped with the saints and tried to survive off the overflow of what others told me about God. Unfortunately, I retained only bits and pieces of the information. It's like when you are a student and you hear the teacher talking, but you don't grasp the concept until you see it for yourself or try it for yourself. The same thing applies when knowing God. The only way to know God is by communing with Him in prayer and meditating on His word. God is so intentional about love that he broke it down for us in 1 Corinthians 13: 4-8.

Love endures with patience and serenity, love is kind and thoughtful, and is not jealous or envious; love does not brag and is not proud or arrogant. It is not rude; it is not self-seeking, it is not provoked [nor overly sensitive and easily angered]; it does not take into account a wrong endured. It does not rejoice at injustice, but rejoices with the truth [when right and truth prevail]. Love bears all things [regardless of what comes], believes all things [looking for the best in each one], hopes all things [remaining steadfast during difficult times], endures all things [without weakening]. Love never fails [it never fades nor ends].

As you can see, love embodies everything that God is to us. We see time and time again that Jesus demonstrated this while He walked this earth. Now you may have read this and immediately tried to apply it to a significant other, but we must first start evaluating ourselves. In order to love others, we must first love God, then we must love ourselves, and finally we can begin to love others.

Keeping It L.I.V.E.

Having gained a true understanding of what love is, take some time to really break down 1 Corinthians 13:4-8. Complete the chart below reviewing the characteristics of love. Then, think about where you fall on a scale of 1-3 and assess how well you have been showing these elements of love. Once you have finished, pray, and complete the reflection questions.

What is Love Chart

Characteristics of Love	**How Am I doing on a scale of 1-3?** **1- HELP Me Lord** **2- Making Progress** **3-I've been Changed**
Endures with patience and serenity	
Is kind and thoughtful	
Is NOT jealous or envious	
Does NOT brag	
Is NOT proud or arrogant	

Is NOT rude	
Is NOT self-seeking	
Is NOT provoked (overly sensitive or easily angered)	
Does NOT take into account a wrong	
Does NOT rejoice at injustice	
Rejoices with truth	
Bears all things	
Believes all things	
Hopes all things	
Endures all things	
Never fails (fades or ends)	

Guiding Prayer:

Heavenly Father,
Thank You for being love. Thank You for loving me unconditionally and consistently. I honor You for showing us how to love You, myself, and others. Father, forgive me for all the times that I have misused love and not loved well. I know that I've been hurt by people who did not love well, so I just want to say I forgive them. I recognize that those who hurt me never truly knew you; therefore, they were not able to love me well. For those I have hurt by not loving them well, I pray that You would forgive me. I pray that my lack of loving them will not hinder them from loving You, themself, and others well. I ask that You help me to love like You. Speak to me throughout the day so that I am aware of the moments when I need to love better. I give You all the honor, power, and glory in Jesus' name, Amen!

Reflection Questions:

1. Why is love so important to God?
2. How does understanding love help me in life?
3. How has my perspective changed since reading 1 Corinthians 13:4-8?
4. What areas do I need to love better?
5. What steps can I take today to love better?

Journal

Day 5

SEXUAL PURITY

Dear Singles,

Abstinence is never to be used as a golden ticket, but more so as a reflection of how we honor God by abstaining from sexual activity until marriage. This is such an important area to discuss because there are many Christian singles who are still sexually active even as virgins. There's a lie that has been going around where people think that because there is no penetration, they are okay. Well let me burst your bubble to help you realize that masturbation, pornography, and doing anything that involves sexual pleasure will draw us further from God. This goes for individuals who are engaged, divorced, and widowed. Until you have stood at the altar or courthouse and legally gotten married, abstinence should be your portion. Many individuals try to use this area as an excuse to not fully commit to God, but what you will find is that we are not as strong as we think we are.

Being involved in sexual acts will cloud your judgement and eventually your desire for it will become stronger than your desire for God. This eventually leads to sexual activity becoming an idol that will eventually hinder your ability to see God in people. Instead, you will find that you will begin to see people through a sexual lens. This type of desire is what has led so many individuals to commit heinous sexual acts that we say we would never do. Pedophilia, rape, incest, adultery, and even murder are all rooted in the lust created by an unhealthy relationship with sex.

In 2 Samuel 11, we gain a different perspective of David. He lusted for Bathsheba so much that he slept with her while her husband was away at war, impregnated her, and then arranged for her husband to be killed. Even David's son Amnon suffered from lust so much that he raped his own sister Tamar in 2 Samuel 13. Those sexual acts driven by lust reaped massive consequences.

As you go through life, you will find that most people who struggle sexually were exposed to sex prematurely through pornography, molestation, and/or sexual abuse. I am an overcomer of sexual abuse, and I can honestly say that being exposed to sex in such an unhealthy manner opened the door for me to indulge in promiscuity. My identity became skewed and lust opened the door for many idols to hinder my ability to seek and honor God.

1 Corinthians 6:12-20 helped me to understand why it is so important to protect myself sexually. It helped me to

understand that sex is not bad, but when performed outside of marriage it opens the doorway for our flesh to crave things that should only be awakened within the covenant of marriage.

Everything is permissible for me, but not all things are beneficial. Everything is permissible for me, but I will not be enslaved by anything [and brought under its power, allowing it to control me]. Food is for the stomach and the stomach for food, but God will do away with both of them. The body is not intended for sexual immorality, but for the Lord, and the Lord is for the body [to save, sanctify, and raise it again because of the sacrifice of the cross]. And God has not only raised the Lord [to life], but will also raise us up by His power. Do you not know that your bodies are members of Christ? Am I therefore to take the members of Christ and make them part of a prostitute? Certainly not! Do you not know that the one who joins himself to a prostitute is one body with her? For He says, "The two shall be one flesh." But the one who is united and joined to the Lord is one spirit with Him. Run away from sexual immorality [in any form, whether thought or behavior, whether visual or written]. Every other sin that a man commits is outside the body, but the one who is sexually immoral sins against his own body. Do you not know that your body is a temple of the Holy Spirit who is within you, whom you have [received as a gift] from God, and that you are not your own [property]? You were bought with a price [you were actually purchased with the precious blood of Jesus and made His own]. So then, honor and glorify God with your body.

Some of you may read this and feel a sense of shame or guilt, but I ask that you simply make a commitment to make a change. Others of you may say you're a virgin so this doesn't apply, well I must inform you that you must be mindful of what you allow yourself to watch, listen to, and even discuss. Remain humble and do not be boastful in doing what we are all called to do in reverence to God. Instead, invest in encouraging others to remain sexually pure.

Keeping It L.I.V.E.

As a Christian single, we are often told not to have sex without understanding the repercussions of doing such a thing. No matter what experiences you have had with sex, meditate on 1 Corinthians 6:12-20. Pray to God and allow Him to share His heart with you regarding this area of your life. It may seem minute, but sexual purity allows us to have clear judgement when making decisions, including choosing our spouse. So, choose today to commit or recommit your sexuality to God knowing that abstinence is to help you and not to harm you.

Guiding Prayer:

Heavenly Father,
Thank You for creating sex and constantly reminding me why it is important to refrain from it until marriage. I repent for engaging in any activity or conversation that arouses me and causes my thoughts to run rampant and far from You. Lord give me the strength to remain pure and the discernment and wisdom to stay away from those who would try to tempt me and cause me harm. Lord help me to honor You with my body so that I may continue to walk in the abundance of Your will for my life. I give You all the honor, power, and glory in Jesus' name, Amen!

Reflection Questions:

1. Why is it important to remain sexually pure?
2. What has been my experience with sex?
3. Who do I have in my life that is biblically sound and available to hold me accountable in this area?
4. What things do I need to stop watching, listening to, and talking about to help me refrain from thinking about sex?
5. What purposeful activities can I engage in to help me remain focused?

Journal

Day 6

SUBMISSION

Dear Singles,

During the season of singleness, we are blessed with the opportunity of making ourselves a priority, not above God though. Typically, people see this as an opportunity to do whatever they want whenever they want, but I've come to realize that even in that there is the danger of growing selfish, entitled, and stubborn. Submission is a word that is often used in regard to women being submitted to men which is a statement taken out of context. Ephesians 5 clearly states that husbands are to be submitted to their wives, and wives are to be submitted to their husbands. Now, there is One who men and women should remain submitted to in every season and that my friend is God. Submission to God is what helps us embrace singleness in a healthy way. It allows us to live intentionally and victoriously because we honestly cannot go wrong submitting every aspect of our lives to God. We shouldn't live for marriage, but we should recognize that how we live in our singleness has the ability to hinder or enhance our marriage.

As a single, I had been told what to do so many times, but I quickly realized that if God hadn't approved it then it was going to be more of a burden than a blessing. Proverbs 19:21 is very clear about how we can make our own plans, but only plans submitted to God will prevail.

Many plans are in a man's mind, But it is the Lord's purpose for him that will stand (be carried out).

I'm reminded of Jesus, who didn't do anything without God granting him permission to do so. All the miracles, signs, and wonders were done with submission to God. In the same way, He made sure He did what was required of Him even if it was painful. Jesus understood the heart, plan, and principles of God. For instance, in Matthew 26: 36-41, while in the Garden of Gethsemane, Jesus asked God if He could avoid having to be crucified, but He still submitted to God's Will.

Then Jesus came with them to a place called Gethsemane (olive-press), and He told His disciples, "Sit here while I go over there and pray." And taking with Him Peter and the two sons of Zebedee [James and John], He began to be grieved and greatly distressed. Then He said to them, "My soul is deeply grieved, so that I am almost dying of sorrow. Stay here and stay awake and keep watch with Me." And after going a little farther, He fell face down and prayed, saying, "My Father, if it is possible [that is, consistent with Your will], let this cup pass from Me; yet not as I will, but as You will." And He came to the disciples and found them sleeping, and said to Peter, "So, you men could not stay awake and keep watch with Me for one hour? Keep actively watching and praying that you may not come into temptation; the spirit is willing, but the body is weak."

He went away a second time and prayed, saying, "My Father, if this cannot pass away unless I drink it, Your will be done." Again He came and found them sleeping, for their eyes were heavy. So, leaving them again, He went away and prayed for the third time, saying the same words once more.

In a world that thrives off Y.O.L.O. (You Only Live Once), I choose to promote that we only live for the Kingdom and doing that is enough to ensure that we will live a life that's pleasing to God and beneficial to our development.

Keeping It L.I.V.E.

Consider the plans that you have made for your life. You may have said you will be married by a specific time, that you will buy a house, move to a new city, or travel overseas. Whatever the case may be, I challenge you to meditate on Proverbs 19:21 and ask God about those plans. Pray and reflect on what He says.

Guiding Prayer:

Heavenly Father,

Thank You for being the author and foundation of my life. Lord, I recognize that in the past I may not have consulted You regarding the plans I have created. I repent for trying to live my life according to my plans and I ask that You help me to submit every area of my life to You. Father, speak to me loud and clearly so that I may not pursue the things that You do not will for me. If there are doors that I've opened outside of Your will, please shut them and help me to recognize the doors that You have opened for me. Lord I love You, and I'm committed to living a life submitted to Your will and Your way. I give You all the honor, power, and glory in Jesus' name, Amen!

Reflection Questions:

1. What does submitting to Christ look like for me?
2. What goals and plans have I made?
3. How do they align with the purpose and plans God has for me?
4. What plans and goals will I need to put aside?

Journal

Day 7

HEALING

Dear Singles,

As human beings, we come from various types of backgrounds and experiences. Some of those experiences may not have been as pleasant as others. Unfortunately, we aren't always aware of the impact negative experiences can have on our life until we connect with other people. Quite a few marriages have ended as a result of unhealed places not being dealt with. I always think about what those unions would have been like if they had begun the healing process prior to getting married.

I've been involved in relationships and soon found that certain words and actions triggered areas within my own life that were not healed. Then, I've met men who themselves had not healed from past hurts, so they began to project their own pain. The most dangerous place to be is in denial of the need to be healed. We are in an era where the need for therapy is a must. The phrase "hurt people hurt people" rings truer than ever when it comes to relationships in any capacity. During our single season, we should invest in our spiritual, emotional, and mental wellness. Although we have mental illness on the rise, we must not forget that there is a spiritual root to everything that manifests in the natural.

We can surely partner with a biblically sound spiritual leader for help, but even with deliverance we need to partner with medically trained professionals to help us strategically unlearn the bad habits that are learned as a result of trauma. The beauty of being a follower of Christ is that Christ believed in healing. In fact, Isaiah 53:5 reminds us that He died so that we could receive spiritual, physical, emotional, and mental healing.

But He was wounded for our transgressions, He was crushed for our wickedness [our sin, our injustice, our wrongdoing]; The punishment [required] for our well-being fell on Him, And by His stripes (wounds) we are healed.

In Matthew, Mark, Luke, and John we gain much insight into the importance of healing. Jesus just needed those who received healing to believe even though Jesus performed great miracles such as raising individuals from the dead, healing physical ailments, and delivering individuals from demonic spirits that hindered their ability function.

Along with healing, we have to discuss the importance of forgiveness. Many of us don't realize that much of our emotional and physical illnesses are rooted in unforgiveness. Unforgiveness is a slow killer. The harmful things people do against us is not right, but holding unforgiveness hurts us more than it hurts them. Ultimately, our inability to forgive causes us to put up barriers that hinder us from authentically connecting with God and others. Proverbs 17:9 is a testament of how unforgiveness blocks our ability to love and that creates division.

He who covers and forgives an offense seeks love, But he who repeats or gossips about a matter separates intimate friends.

A few years ago, I went through a season of spiritual and emotional torment. I needed to do some heart work and one of the scriptures that resonated with me so powerfully was Psalm 51:10.

Create in me a clean heart, O God, And renew a right and steadfast spirit within me.

Be intentional about doing the healing work today because the plan God has for you depends on it.

Keeping It L.I.V.E.

Today's devotional will need to be revisited often. Every day we experience offenses, whether received or given. Either way we need to be intentional about acknowledging the healing that needs to take place within ourselves. Take some time today meditating on the scriptures above, praying to God, and reflecting on the questions.

Guiding Prayer:

Heavenly Father,
Thank You for being my healer. Thank You for ensuring that I don't harbor anger, resentment, resentment and unforgiveness. Lord I surrender all offenses made against me to You. I forgive those who have harmed me verbally, mentally, emotionally, and/or physically. Father I know that You will vindicate me for those who have wronged me. So, I ask that You forgive me and heal my heart and mind so that I can move forward. Father, I thank You that You are restoring me and bringing healthy people into my life. I pray that You help me to recognize moments when I am hurting so that I run to You rather than projecting them on other people. Lord I also pray that You guide me to the spiritual and natural support that I need to overcome past trauma known and unknown. Father I declare and decree that I am healed. I give You all the honor, power, and glory in Jesus' name, Amen!

Reflection Questions:

1. Why is it important to invest in my healing?
2. What negative experiences have I encountered in the past or recently?
3. How do I feel about those involved?
4. What steps have I taken towards forgiving those individuals?
5. What accountability and support system do I have in my life to support me when I am experiencing emotional, physical, spiritual, or mental pain?
6. Have my relationships been impacted by any of the past hurts I've experienced?
7. Reflect on past relationships whether they were romantic or platonic. What behavioral patterns have I recognized?
8. How do I envision myself healed?
9. How do I envision healthy healed relationships in my life?

Journal

Day 8

POSITIONING

Dear Singles,

I know we are used to being told that we need to look a certain way, go to certain places, and do certain things to meet someone and transition from singleness to marriage. I'm all for self-development, but the mindset behind doing these things needs to be for you and not to get someone. Being positioned goes deeper than us manipulating people and situations to get recognized or get what we want. Our greatest way of being positioned is by consistently cultivating a relationship with God, obeying His instruction, having sound counsel, and men intentionally pursuing while women are responding well.

I've met quite a few singles who have been single for so long that the mere talk of marriage is detestable to them. Most will say it was because they grew up in a place where marriage was not taught in an admirable way. Instead, it was taught as if it had to be pursued and there was a certain level of perfection that had to be attained to reach that point. Over the last few years, I've been very intentional about asking Godly married and engaged couples questions about their journey from singleness to marriage. The beauty of their stories is that none of them were perfect, but all of them involved each individual being strategically positioned by God.

We are in an era where men and women have been improperly positioned. There are women pursuing men even to the point of proposing marriage. Men were designed to recognize and pursue. Women were designed to respond. In both cases, choice is involved but when making decisions we must use the leading of the Holy Spirit, wisdom, and discernment to make such a critical decision. Let's consider Ruth and Boaz.

I know many individuals love to reference the story of Ruth and Boaz which I find to be admirable as well, but let's just think about how Ruth and Boaz were both properly positioned. Ruth was working and honoring her mother in law while Boaz was being the businessman that he was. Ruth had committed to serving Christ, and Boaz was already serving Christ. Ruth had someone who poured into her, and Boaz had a community among family and friends. I find it interesting that Ruth unknowingly went to glean in Boaz's field. Some may call it coincidence, but when we serve a sovereign God, I can't help but say it was intentionality. In Ruth 2:1-20, we see that as Ruth worked in Boaz's field and Boaz checked on his field, they were both positioned to meet each other.

Now Naomi had a relative of her husband, a man of great wealth and influence, from the family of Elimelech, whose name was Boaz. And Ruth the Moabitess said to Naomi, "Please let me go to the field and glean among the ears of grain after one [of the reapers] in whose sight I may find favor." Naomi said to her, "Go, my daughter." So Ruth went and picked up the leftover grain in a field after the reapers; and she happened to stop at the plot of land belonging to Boaz, who was of the family of Elimelech. It was then that Boaz came back from Bethlehem and said to the reapers, "The Lord be with you!" And they answered him, "The Lord bless you!" Then Boaz said to his servant who was in charge of the reapers, "Whose young woman is this?" The servant in charge of the reapers answered, "She is the young Moabite woman who came back with Naomi from the country of Moab. And she said, 'Please let me glean and gather after the reapers among the sheaves.' So she came and has continued [gathering grain] from early morning until now, except when she sat [resting] for a little while in the [field] house." Then Boaz said to Ruth, "Listen carefully, my daughter. Do not go to glean in another field or leave this one, but stay here close by my maids. Watch which field they reap, and follow behind them. I have commanded the servants not to touch you. And when you are thirsty, go to the [water] jars and drink from what the servants draw." Then she kneeled face downward, bowing to the ground, and said to him, "Why have I found favor in your eyes that you should notice me, when I am a foreigner?" Boaz answered her, "I have been made fully aware of everything that you have done for your mother-in-law since the death of your husband, and how you have left your father and mother and the land of your birth, and have come to a people that you did not know before. May the Lord repay you for your kindness, and may your reward be full from the Lord, the God of Israel, under whose wings you have come to take refuge." Then she said, "Let me find favor in your sight, my lord, for you have comforted me and have spoken kindly to your maidservant, though I am not as one of your maidservants." At mealtime Boaz said to her, "Come over here and eat some bread and dip your bread in the vinegar." So she sat beside the reapers; and he served her roasted grain, and she ate until she was satisfied and she had some left [for Naomi]. When she got up to glean, Boaz ordered his servants, "Let her glean even among the sheaves, and do not insult her. Also you shall purposely pull out for her some stalks [of grain] from the sheaves and leave them so that she may collect them, and do not rebuke her." So she gleaned in the field until evening. Then she beat out what she had gleaned, and it was about an ephah of barley. She picked it up and went into the city, and her mother-in-law saw what she had gleaned. Ruth also took out and gave to Naomi what she had saved after she [had eaten and] was sat-

isfied. Her mother-in-law said to her, "Where did you glean today? Where did you work? Blessed be the man who took notice of you." So she told her mother-in-law with whom she had worked and said, "The name of the man with whom I worked today is Boaz." Naomi said to her daughter-in-law, "May he be blessed of the Lord who has not ceased His kindness to the living and to the dead." Again Naomi said to her, "The man is one of our closest relatives, one who has the right to redeem us."

I'm aware that many individuals have started to pervert the actions of Ruth in chapter 3, but I want us to focus on the fact that after Boaz acknowledged Ruth in the field, Ruth responded by getting dressed up and going to Boaz's threshing floor. Boaz confirmed his interest by protecting her reputation, and she did not go back home empty handed. Under the instruction of her mother in law, Ruth was simply told to wait while Boaz got his affairs in order. In chapter 4, Boaz received approval to marry Ruth and it was a done deal.

Keeping It L.I.V.E.

In our desire for marriage, we often have to consider if we have positioned ourselves well for marriage. There are many practical things that can be done, but even in that the root of it has to be led by the Holy Spirit. Spend some time praying and asking God to reveal ways that you can be properly positioned. Then, use the reflection questions to further identify the areas of development you can focus on to build yourself.

Guiding Prayer:

Heavenly Father,
Thank You for Your omniscience. Father You desire to see me thrive in every area of my life and I'm trusting You to guide me in all things. Lord, show me the areas of development and growth that I need to experience so that I am well positioned for what or who You have for me. Open my eyes and mind to recognize and receive the good things and people You have in store for me. Lord I also ask that You surround me with sound and wise counselors who can provide assistance as I am being positioned. I give You all the honor, power, and glory in Jesus' name, Amen!

Reflection Questions:

1. What areas of self-development have I been working on?
2. Who has God placed in my life to be sound and wise counsel for me?
3. How does the story of Ruth and Boaz impact my thought process on being well positioned for marriage?
4. What is God telling me to do to ensure I am being positioned well?

Journal

Day 9

COMMUNITY (FRIENDSHIP/ACCOUNTABILITY)

Dear Singles,

*A*s an individual, we must learn how to function in community with friends and accountability. I've met quite a few singles who despise accountability and have not embraced the beauty of friendship. I think it was so strategic of God to emphasize friendship more than marriage. We sometimes underestimate the impact our friends and who we surround ourselves with has on the decisions we make and the way we think. Proverbs is full of wisdom regarding friendships and being mindful of the individuals we choose to surround ourselves with.

Proverbs 22: 24-25

Do not even associate with a man given to angry outbursts; Or go [along] with a hot-tempered man, Or you will learn his [undisciplined] ways And get yourself trapped [in a situation from which it is hard to escape].

Proverbs 13:20

He who walks [as a companion] with wise men will be wise, But the companions of [conceited, dull-witted] fools [are fools themselves and] will experience harm.

Proverbs 18:24

The man of too many friends [chosen indiscriminately] will be broken in pieces and come to ruin, But there is a [true, loving] friend who [is reliable and] sticks closer than a brother.

What I have found is that my friends are all very different from me, but the one thing we have in common is our love for Christ. I often tell people that the friends you have are often a source of preparation for your spouse. When in community we are challenged to love unconditionally, forgive quickly and frequently, communicate effectively, and operate with transparency and authenticity.

Our community also tends to be the eyes and ears for us. We all have blind spots and need people who can see things that we may be overlooking. Proverbs also provides scripture on how beneficial our friends can be when it comes to needing spiritual accountability and support during adversity.

Proverbs 17:17

A friend loves at all times, And a brother is born for adversity.

Proverbs 27:17

As iron sharpens iron, So one man sharpens [and influences] another [through discussion].

Another element of being in community is being able to have healthy platonic relationships with the opposite sex. I'll admit that at one point in life, I didn't want any more male friends unless they were my husband. I soon realized that I was contradicting myself because I genuinely desired for my husband to be my best friend. After observing Jesus and the importance of friendships, I soon realized that I had allowed negative experiences to create a generalization about men having the inability to be true friends. The issue was that the men I had encountered weren't true men of God. Therefore, they never had the capacity to be true friends.

I've observed that when we ignore friendship whether the relationship becomes romantic or not, we are missing opportunities to gain relationships that will help us fulfill Kingdom tasks that God desires for us to fulfill. I think about the many relationships that were damaged because men and women rushed to be romantically involved without seeking to be in community with each other.

Community is a blessing that affords us with opportunities to gain amazing Godly friendships and accountability that will help us to not maneuver through life alone. Jesus had the disciples and the disciples had each other. So, be mindful of your community understanding that it matters in singleness and marriage.

Keeping It L.I.V.E.

You may have someone or a few individuals in mind that you would love to connect with on a romantic level, but I challenge you to spend today focusing on friendship. First consider your own friendships, then reflect on the friendships of those you may be interested in. Pray and ask God to make you a better friend while also connecting you with better friends.

Guiding Prayer:

Heavenly Father,
Thank You for being a true friend. Thank You for showing me what it looks like to have accountability and support. I ask that You help me to be a better friend to those You've entrusted to me. In the same way, I ask that You remove those who cause harm to me and add friends who genuinely love You and desire to see Your will for our lives manifest. Father, I pray that as I wait for my spouse that you would allow me

to not rush to developing a romantic relationship. Help us to pursue You in friendship and when the time is right You will allow us to see each other as more than friends. I give You all the honor, power, and glory in Jesus' name, Amen!

Reflection Questions:

1. Why is friendship important in singleness?
2. Who are my friends?
3. What are common factors between me and my friends?
4. What types of discussions do my friends and I have?
5. Are my friends pursuing Christ?
6. Have I been a loyal, loving, and honest friend?
7. Do I have any friends of the opposite sex?
8. What differences do my friends and I have?
9. What type of friends do I desire to have?

Journal

Day 10

PURPOSE OVER PREFERENCE

Dear Singles,

*W*hen purpose outweighs preference you walk into a union full of pleasure versus pain!

How many times have we allowed ourselves to be in relationships because it was convenient, or the other person embodied a few qualities we like? If God created us for purpose, why wouldn't He position us to become one with someone for purpose? Rather than understanding our own purpose and positioning ourselves to be with someone who shares a connected purpose, we stop at "Well, they're saved, go to church, read the Bible, and pray." [Note: Every saved man or woman will not be God's best for you.] Or, we place more value on their looks, job, nationality, economic status, friends, or other things that we'd prefer to have in a mate. Considering these things is great, but we have to seek God to see the whole picture of how that person's position in our lives will align with God's plan for our lives.

In Matthew 6:33, we are instructed to *seek first the kingdom of God and his righteousness, and all these things will be added to you.* Our number 1 priority is God and His will for our lives. By placing God first, we surrender our desires and preferences to His desires and preferences for us. Psalm 37:4 tells us *to delight [ourselves] in the Lord, and he will give [us] the desires of [our] heart.* Knowing this and remembering that God has already established a plan for our lives that gives us hope and a future (Jeremiah 29:11) is all the more reason we should consider purpose over preference when choosing a mate.

I'm well aware many are waiting and the wait could be a result of you or your mate being developed and repositioned, but please be wise and intentional as you keep your eyes out for those sent your way. If there is absolutely no confirmation of how you and this person's purposes connect, then be okay with walking away and allowing God to continue to be your matchmaker. God wants to create unions that glorify Him and further the Kingdom of Heaven on Earth. So, no matter how inconvenient the wait is to your emotions, trust God and know that He knows who is best for you!

Keeping It L.I.V.E.

As much as people have been told to not make a list, I believe that there is a list that can be written down when partnered with the Holy Spirit. When we partner with the Holy Spirit and read our Word, He will begin to reveal things to us about ourselves and He will highlight attributes that will be suitable for us. Today, you will spend time worshipping God, reading the Word of God, and searching the Scripture for attributes you'd like to see in your spouse. Then, write down whatever the Holy Spirit reveals to you. The Holy Spirit may not reveal everything at once, so keep this journal entry close so that you are able to update it.

Guiding Prayer:

Heavenly Father,
Thank you for being intentional with how You've created me. Father forgive me for allowing myself to think I know what and who is best for me. Lord purify my heart and mind of lust and every fleshly desire that is preventing me from seeing who I need in my life. As I spend time with You, I ask that You remove the scales from my eyes and help me to see the attributes of the spouse You would have for me. Father give me vision for the purpose you have created for me and

my future spouse. Help me to not be shallow, judgmental, or limited in perspective. Guide me to recognize good fruit and what that would look like in the life of my Kingdom spouse. Father, I surrender my desires to You believing that You know what I need and that You have someone suitable for me. Lord, as I actively wait for my spouse and I to connect, I ask that You would help me to become the suitable spouse I need to be. I give You all the honor, power, and glory in Jesus' name, Amen!

Reflection Questions:

1. What am I attracted to in the opposite sex?
2. How do these qualities align with the calling on my life?
3. What are my preferences as it pertains to my future spouse?
4. How do I reflect those preferences?
5. Are any of the preferences I've listed carnal or flesh minded?
6. Do I have fears regarding who my spouse will be?
7. Why do I have these fears?
8. What scriptures can I confess to overcome these fears?

Journal

Day 11

MARRIAGE

Dear Singles,

*D*esiring marriage is not a sin. If you desire marriage, then I'm sure God planted that seed within you and there is absolutely nothing wrong with that. Marriage is a beautiful representation of how Christ loves the Church, but many individuals and institutions have perverted marriage or made it an idol. Quite a few singles have either lost hope in seeing Godly marriages or simply lost hope in the institution of marriage itself. There are many singles who have been waiting for years and even decades. Many have been told there was something wrong with them but let me be the first to free you from that mindset. Marriage is possible, but if you are reading this book, I believe you don't desire to have just any marriage. You desire to have a covenant Godly marriage that glorifies God.

The weight of marriage is heavy and should not be taken lightly. Women and men both play a significant role, but due to dysfunction of the world the roles of men and women have often been reversed. I'm not talking about domestic tasks, but Kingdom roles within marriage. When the topic of relationships comes up, I've observed that many are asked, "Are you a Proverbs 31 woman and are you an Ephesians 5 man?" I understand the Proverbs 31 concept. It is a great guide, full of wisdom that is beneficial to women and men looking for a Godly woman. One thing I never truly understood is why people would always ask a man whether or not he was an Ephesians 5 man as if Ephesians 5 was directed to men only. With me having an inquiring mind, I decided to go back to Ephesians 5 and really consider who was speaking and who was being spoken to.

Ephesians 5:1 tells us that Ephesians was written by Apostle Paul to the saints (believers of Christ) of Ephesus. I noticed that it wasn't limited to male or female, but rather the WHOLE body of Christ. The way Ephesians 5 is organized is very strategic. Think about it, before there is ever an us or we, there was a you and me. Meaning before we connect with someone to become one, we must become whole as individuals making sure we have submitted to Christ first. Before Paul discusses how wives and husbands should love each other, he gives a thorough explanation on how we as believers should walk in love just like Christ.

Therefore become imitators of God [copy Him and follow His example], as well-beloved children [imitate their father]; ² and walk continually in love [that is, value one another—practice empathy and compassion, unselfishly seeking the best for others], just as Christ also loved you and gave Himself up for us, an offering and sacrifice to God [slain for you, so that it became] a sweet fragrance.
Ephesians 5:1-2

Paul opens this chapter by explaining that we should selflessly love like God showing empathy and being compassionate towards others. In Ephesians 5:3-21, he breaks down what walking in love looks like. For instance, he emphasizes how we should live a sexually pure lifestyle, refrain from all filthy/ungodly speech and behavior, be the light in the midst of darkness (be IN the world NOT OF the world), use wisdom and discernment, don't get drunk, and always be in a state of thanksgiving. Paul makes sure that we understand that our first commitment is to Christ and submitting to His will and His way. Now, in Ephesians 5:22-33 Paul speaks to us regarding how to love our spouse.

Wives, be subject to your own husbands, as [a service] to the Lord. For the husband is head of the wife, as Christ is head of the church, Himself being the Savior of the body. But as the church is subject to Christ, so also wives should be subject to

their husbands in everything [respecting both their position as protector and their responsibility to God as head of the house].
Ephesians 5:22-24

What I love about this section is that it's about so much more than a man being a husband; it educates us on the hierarchy of matrimonial love. God is the head of the relationship and the husband and wife submit to God FIRST and then to each other. The remaining verses go on to discuss how a husband should love his wife like *Christ loved the church and give himself up for her* (Ephesians 5:25). That level of love is equivalent to completely sacrificing oneself for the benefit of someone else similar to Jesus sacrificing his life for the Church (believers of Christ). After going more in depth regarding how men should love their wives, Paul leaves us with *let the wife see that she respects her husband* (Ephesians 5:33). I find it interesting how Paul emphasizes a husband loving his wife and a wife respecting her husband. It just goes to show that as the head of a household, the husband must pour out the love he has embraced from God. This takes me to the importance of husbands really embracing God as their Father and Lover of their soul. A husband can't love a wife if he hasn't received love from the Creator of love. He wouldn't be able to lead with the power and authority Christ gave unless he first submitted and allowed himself to learn how to operate in the power and authority of Christ. Likewise, a wife cannot love unless she has accepted God's love. Just like she cannot respect her husband until she has learned what it's like to be respected by God as her Father.

Ephesians 5 is a very simple, yet vivid illustration of what the process of love should look like in our lives as individuals and then as one with our spouse. The covenant of marriage is not for the faint of heart, but it's not impossible if you have Christ at the center of the union.

Keeping It L.I.V.E.

Understanding the purpose of marriage is imperative for those who desire to marry. Ephesians 5 creates a clear picture of how God designed it to look and it's evident that husbands carry a significant weight just as Christ carries the weight of the church. This doesn't mean wives are off the hook. How wives and husbands love has the capacity to make or break a union. Read and meditate on Ephesians 5 and pray it over your future marriage. Also, reflect on areas that you believe God is highlighting to you in preparation for such a union. Take some time to pray and listen to God's heart as it relates to marriage for you and don't be afraid to search the Bible for additional scriptures on marriage (i.e., 1 Corinthians 7).

Guiding Prayer:

Heavenly Father,
I thank You for creating the institution of marriage. Forgive those who have perverted the covenant of marriage. Lord I have the desire to marry, but I want to ensure that I do not make it an idol. If I have made it an idol, I ask that you forgive me and realign my focus towards you. Help me to understand that I exist for your glory, so even if I never get married, I will remain at peace because I have You. Lord, I pray that when the time comes for me to marry that You will give me the wisdom and strength to choose according to the biblical expectation that You have created for a Godly husband or wife. As I wait, I ask that You mold me into the Godly spouse I need to be for a spouse that is suitable for me. I give You all the honor, power, and glory in Jesus' name, Amen!

Reflection Questions:

1. What is the purpose of marriage?
2. Why do I desire to be married?
3. What will I do if I don't get married?
4. How has my perspective on marriage changed or enhanced since reading Ephesians 5?
5. What Godly marriages inspire me and why?

Journal

Word to the Wise

As a single, we must develop in wisdom. I've fasted and prayed for years for God to fill me with wisdom and it has helped me evade many situations that would have derailed me on my journey towards waiting well. I've compiled a series of writings simply offering Godly wisdom to you all. My sole purpose in life is to embrace the broken-hearted, educate the lost, and empower the hopeless. I pray that you are empowered and encouraged to not grow weary in the waiting, understanding that God has a plan in store for you.

Meditate on the scriptures below and apply the wisdom I've provided to your everyday life. Stay hopeful and remember that we must keep God at the center of all seasons.

James 1:5

If any of you lacks wisdom [to guide him through a decision or circumstance], he is to ask of [our benevolent] God, who gives to everyone generously and without rebuke or blame, and it will be given to him.

Proverbs 19:20

Listen to counsel, receive instruction, and accept correction, That you may be wise in the time to come.

Proverbs 18:15

The mind of the prudent [always] acquires knowledge,

And the ear of the wise [always] seeks knowledge.

Psalm 111:10

The [reverent] fear of the Lord is the beginning (the prerequisite, the absolute essential, the alphabet) of wisdom; A good understanding and a teachable heart are possessed by all those who do the will of the Lord; His praise endures forever.

Ecclesiastes 7:12

For wisdom is a protection even as money is a protection, But the [excellent] advantage of knowledge is that wisdom shields and preserves the lives of its possessors.

Dear Singles,

Marriage is not a reward for obedience.

Marriage is not a destination.

Marriage is a new assignment on the timeline of your life that was created to add to your journey towards fulfilling God's purpose for your life.

There's this little myth floating around that tells singles that we are ready for marriage when we take care of ourselves mentally and emotionally, workout, eat healthy, get our finances in order, walk in purpose, travel, be social, and live a life yielded to God. What's not being told is that marriage is not a reward or a destination. It's an addition to the plan God has already established for our life. It has no deadline and any healthy spirit-led person knows that it will happen when God says it's time. Of course, anyone can be married, but there is a very big difference between a union formed under God's covering and one created by our own desire.

I say this to remind singles to not be distracted by what has not yet been released in our lives. I know it's not easy and having everyone tell us what to do to make it to marriage becomes a distraction from what God may need us to focus on in this season.

Heart to Heart: I know what it's like to see others experience their love story, but please don't allow anyone to make you feel as if you are the reason for your singleness. Singleness is not a curse, punishment, or indication that something is wrong with you. I know many who are married and were very far from prepared when it happened, and then there are singles who are thriving with not even one prospect. Both cases are gentle reminders that as much as we would like to think we control the situation, those submitted to God know that it often boils down to God's timing.

I wish I could give you concrete answers as to why the timing differs, but all I can say is that even God's timing is intentional and related to the plan He has for our lives. Understand that as people, we all have assignments that must be accomplished individually. For those who are called to marriage, they are given a new assignment that involves another person. Together they will continue their journey towards fulfilling God's purpose. So, once again, don't panic, don't grow weary, don't allow others to make you think less of yourself, and don't be anxious or stress yourself out trying to make marriage happen. Remember the purpose of marriage and invest in yourself to become the best for you and the assignments God needs to fulfill through you!

Dear Singles,

Being content in singleness doesn't mean we need to fill emotional voids by befriending people of the opposite sex to meet needs that should only be met by God and your future spouse. Boundaries matter, create and implement them immediately!!!

Dear Singles,

Never allow a failed relationship to determine your value. Refrain from giving it the power to diminish the Godly relationship revealed through your visions and dreams. Let the peace of God, which surpasses all understanding, guard your hearts and minds (Philippians 4:7). Remember no matter how it ended, God will move in a way that brings you joy and allows Him to be glorified.

Dear Singles,

How you handle your friendships will give you a glimpse into how you'll handle your spouse. So, during your single season, value friendships, improve your communication skills, be receptive to correction, forgive, apologize, intercede in prayer, be selfless, and be more considerate of others. I know you desire marriage, but even in marriage you need friendship, so learn to be a good friend! Who knows, you may be such a good friend that one of them may become your spouse. Just a thought!

Dear Singles,

Grace is not tolerating spiritual, emotional, physical, sexual, financial, or verbal abuse. Let that individual be healed in, with, and through Christ and not you! Yes, pray for them, but remember you are no one's savior. Leave no room to regress into the state of brokenness that God delivered you from. May the scales fall from the eyes of those who have been manipulated or been the manipulator in relationships in Jesus' name, Amen!

Dear Singles,

God's best for you does not equate to perfection. We all have flaws, but please pay attention to an individual's commitment to make progress. Observe and truly reflect on whether you've been graced to walk alongside that person on their journey towards growth and in the same way consider whether or not they will do the same for you. Self-awareness, commitment, and having a teachable spirit are all necessary non-negotiables for ourselves and marital prospects. Pay attention, pray, assess, and be honest with where you are and where they are.

Dear Singles,

If you don't know your calling, the only one you should be calling is Jesus. Our existence on this Earth is greater than marriage. Individually, we have all been created to fulfill a calling that was chosen for us well in advance. Pursue Christ and in that your calling will be revealed which will actually help to better identify a spouse suitable for you.

Know God

Know Thyself

Know Others

In that order!

Dear Singles,

Acknowledge the desire to be married. Just don't idolize it. Many singles are shamed for having a desire for marriage. Quite a few fall into a state of being afraid to even voice that they actually desire to be married. Please understand that

God gave you the desire of marriage. Therefore, you should never be afraid or ashamed to admit that you want to be married. Now, we must take that desire to the One who gave it to us...God! By doing this, we save ourselves from idolizing the idea of marriage. On a practical level, I recommend you journal about your desire. Find scriptures that focus on marriage and ask God to prepare you according to His word and His will for your marriage. Begin to pray for your spouse and if God sends Godly couples into your life begin to observe and glean from them. This should not replace communing with God and continuously building intimacy with him. When you find yourself going to God just for marriage while neglecting His instructions regarding other areas of your life, you've allowed it to become an idol. When you study your Word only in regard to marriage and not for knowing God Himself, you've allowed it to become an idol. God desires a relationship with us, and He will not allow anything or anyone to come before Him. So yes, have the desire, but make sure that your strongest desire is to know and honor Christ, become more like Christ, and to fulfill the will He has for your life first.

Dear Singles,

There comes a time in your development when you walk confidently in who God says He made you to be. Recognize that you are a treasure and you are a phenomenal blessing that is worthy of being valued, respected, and loved. Don't shrink back, dim your light, or settle. Keep shining, thriving, growing, and expecting greatness. Even in the process of growing, we can be confident that we are amazing. It's not an arrogance, but an awareness of the greatness that God created within us. Our awareness of God and self, commitment to making progress, and perseverance to fulfilling purpose is what makes us a prize! Remain humble never looking down on another while also walking with your head up having confidence in Christ and who He created you to be!

Dear Singles,

There are many of us who will never experience some of the challenges others have faced or are facing in their marriage because we chose to steward our single season well. Be okay with not rushing into the married season knowing that God is protecting us from the mistakes we often see others make by moving into marriage prematurely. Embrace this season, listen, glean, and obey when God says move or stay! Trust God knows what's best for you and move at his pace! His 'not yet' comes from a place of him knowing us better than we know ourselves. Use this time to grow and become who He needs you to be just as He prepares your spouse to be who they need to be for you!

Dear Singles,

Don't treat people like they're disposable. If you're not interested leave them alone, let them go, and carry on! Don't over-spiritualize wasting people's time! Be mindful of how you handle God's children. They may not be the one for you, but they are everything and more to somebody else.

Dear Singles,

Pray the hard prayer and ask God to remove anyone and anything that would hinder you from walking in the fullness He created you to flow in. Then, thank Him for the abrupt exposures and removals that have and will take place. It may hurt a little, but it will save you years of pain that would have caused greater damage. Be okay with doing things His way. The exposure, the rejection, the ghosting, and the revelation were all for your good. Remember, God is for us and not against us. His plans are never to harm us, but to give us hope and a future (Jeremiah 29:11). Receive his covering and protection!

Dear Singles,

See value in an individual beyond their ability to be your potential spouse. There are dynamic kingdom connections available to be made, but not manifesting simply because you only choose your associations based on physical attraction and self-gratification. Invest in making healthy kingdom connections!

Dear Singles,

Say it with me, "I am NOT forsaken!" Now, prepare to thrive in singleness and enhance your greatness this year! Wait well, seek God, and trust His timing!

Dear Singles,

Stop making "your type" an idol. Attraction is the necessity and it is not limited to "your type." Let's not miss our blessing because they didn't come packaged in the way we thought they should come. God knows what we would like, but He also recognizes that what we need is more important. So, as you pray for a spouse, pray that God would deliver a Godly attractive mate that is suitable for you. All the specifics of "your type" will have you overlooking someone that could possibly be right in front of you. Be open!

Dear Singles,

What you see before marriage is what you get after marriage. Never marry for who they will become, instead marry for who they are and actively aspire to be. Making decisions off of wishes is a dangerous game to play. Most divorcées tell me they knew the union was a no before saying I do, but they chose to believe the individual would change, or they simply chose to see a person that they desired to see rather than accepting who they were. Someone may be great, but sometimes the pieces just won't fit together and that is okay. Don't force a relationship or try to manipulate it because you will ultimately destroy or break yourself and/or them altogether.

Dear Singles,

The thought of them is not always a sign that you should go back to them. Pray for them and continue moving forward. The EX files should never be reopened without consulting God, wise counsel, and seeing evidence of improvement through observation. Sometimes, we delay ourselves by going in circles with individuals that God has already shown us is not His will for us. Have there been couples who managed to come back together? Absolutely, but it definitely took each individual spending time apart, maturing, and gaining clarity of self before moving forward. You don't have to hate them or feel bad covering them in prayer because as a believer in Christ, we are called to pray for all, and those prayers should include speaking blessings over their lives. No seriously, no curses because we reap what we sow, and Lord knows we come into this world overcoming enough battles. So anytime they pop into your head, speak life, pray for them, and continue to pray for yourself to be set free from anything and anyone who may be hindering you from becoming who God needs you to be and/or hindering you from being available to the individual God needs you to be with.

Dear Singles,

One of the most selfish things we can do is expect God to deliver someone who is whole when we aren't willing to do the work to become whole ourselves. When it comes to setting expectations and having a list, I'm very adamant about looking inward first and then making requests. I used to be the one saying he needs to be this, that, and have all these things, but God reminded me that it's selfish to expect Him to deliver someone who is a complete meal while I'm only serving breadcrumbs. It's not to say that it's not possible, but I recognized very soon that the danger in not partnering with

God for my development would lead me to idolizing that man and seeing him as a savior rescuing me from all my problems. One thing that motivated me to reconsider my thought process was having the desire to add to my spouse. I can't offer what I don't have. It's not a matter of trying to be perfect. It's more so about making an effort to invest in my growth and development so that I don't project or bog my spouse down with weight of baggage that should have been released before we said I do. Once again, this is not to say you will not have flaws because we all have them but having a willingness to remove what we can in our singleness is our way of loving God, ourselves, and our future spouse better. So, be selfless, take a step back, and spend some time understanding who you are, whose you are, and begin seeking God for revelation of the things that need to be removed. As you invest more in God and yourself, He will help you fine tune your list so that you will receive, recognize, and choose based upon God's Will and not your baggage.

Dear Singles,

Asking questions presents an opportunity to gain clarity rather than making assumptions which are often misrepresentations of reality. Ask more, assume less.

Dear Singles,

Stay connected with Godly married couples and glean. Whether you have a prospect or not, it never hurts to learn from the lessons others have learned the hard way.

Dear Singles,

Date with intentionality. The recovery process of a broken heart is so draining and sometimes enabling for a person who is constantly being taken advantage of or vice versa. Just imagine how much healthier and happier we would be if we simply asked God yes or no before getting in too deep. It's amazing how we often skip over this and say we need to date numerous people to determine who would be suitable for us, but just as God reveals desires, gifts, and plans for our life He will reveal a suitable spouse.

Dear Singles,

Everyone has been given the gift of choice, so don't become disheartened when you are not chosen. Your weight gain, weight loss, debt, and other flaws don't disqualify you from being married to a Godly individual. Be transparent about where you are, put a plan into place to actively take steps to improve, and allow your prospect to determine whether they can partner with your journey of self-improvement or not.

Dear Singles,

Spirituality is not confirmation that they are following our Lord and Savior Jesus Christ. You better get specific and check their fruit and its root. There are a lot of spiritual things happening that are not aligned to Jesus Christ. The real question is 'who is your spirit submitted to?', because not every spirit is submitted to Jesus Christ. Dig deeper, observe often, listen more, and pay attention!

Dear Singles,

You're spending too much time looking for you in a spouse when you really should be looking for God. Alignment in their relations with God and evidence of God in every aspect of their life is greater than alignment in food, hobbies, and movies. Yes, common interests are cool, but recognize that your spouse has been equipped to partner with you for a purpose and that may not include them liking everything you're interested in!

Dear Singles,

The God in you is attractive to the one who desires to see it cultivated rather than compromised. If your faith in God is a burden to them then it's safe to say they aren't equipped or suitable to handle the God given mantle that you carry. Remember, you're not for everybody and everybody is not for you, and that's okay!

Dear Singles,

Good is cool, but God is better. Don't settle! God's best is not limited to external appearance, common interests, tangible items, and large bank accounts. His best will always deal more with the heart and character of an individual. Many good options will be presented, but there is a heart for God, fruit of the spirit, and purpose alignment tied to God's options. Use discernment, listen to the Holy Spirit, and take heed to what God shows you about a person through his Word. *But the fruit of the Spirit [the result of His presence within us] is love [unselfish concern for others], joy, [inner] peace, patience [not the ability to wait, but how we act while waiting], kindness, goodness, faithfulness, gentleness, self-control. Against such things there is no law. Galatians 5:22-23*

Dear Singles,

Stewarding your single season well is preparing you to steward your future marriage well. It's all connected, so stay focused and make living for Christ intentionally, victoriously, and expectantly a priority! LIVE and steward every season well!

More from Dr. Ashlei N. Evans

Founder of The Ash Exchange International LLC

The Ash Exchange International LLC is operated, by the founder, Dr. Ashlei N. Evans. This organization is dedicated to developing, equipping, and empowering individuals and institutions (i.e., schools and orphanages) in Africa and the African diaspora through Christ-centered content and services. Dr. Evans provides inspirational Christian content such as books, planning and development resources, and words of encouragement. She offers Spiritual and Interpersonal Leadership Coaching which is geared towards partnering with clients to conquer their goals related to Spiritual Growth, Identity, Purpose, Spiritual Gifts, Relationships, Cultural Competence, and Leadership. Dr. Evans also invests in establishing, restructuring, and maintaining Christian schools and orphanages as an Educational Consultant with an emphasis on School Operations & Management, Curriculum & Instruction, Instructional Coaching, Professional Development, Leadership, Cultural Competence, Relationships, Communication, and Christian Education. The Ash Exchange International LLC values community and collaboration; therefore, Dr. Evans partners with other Christian organizations and individuals to provide conferences and workshops that allow participants to gain wisdom and insight based on biblical principles that can be applied in a practical manner.

Publications:
The Ash Exchange: How One Woman's Life Changed When God Exchanged His Beauty for Her Ashes

Biblical Literacy in a Secular World: Secondary Students' Perceptions of the Influence of Biblical Practices on Academic Achievement

Co-authored Projects:
Tying the Knot Between Ministry and the Marketplace Volume 2
Compiler: Deborah D. Taylor

Available Services:
Spiritual & Interpersonal Leadership Coaching
Educational Consulting
Speaking & Workshop Facilitation
Connect with Dr. Ashlei N. Evans for your next event:
Website: www.TheAshExchange.com
Facebook: www.Facebook.com/DrAshleiNEvans
Instagram: www.Instagram.com/DrAshleiNEvans
Email: TheAshExchange@gmail.com

www.ingramcontent.com/pod-product-compliance
Lightning Source LLC
Chambersburg PA
CBHW030912080526
44589CB00010B/266